CW01149241

Original title:
Words Unspoken

Copyright © 2024 Swan Charm
All rights reserved.

Author: Aron Pilviste
ISBN HARDBACK: 978-9916-79-102-8
ISBN PAPERBACK: 978-9916-79-103-5
ISBN EBOOK: 978-9916-79-104-2

Flickers of the Inarticulate

Words hide away, softly they weep,
In shadows where silence seems deep.
A flicker of thought, just out of grasp,
Caught in the moment, too frail to clasp.

Between whispered dreams and lingering sighs,
Emotions dance, yet remain disguised.
In the quiet, they yearn to be known,
But silence holds tight to the seeds they've sown.

Under the moon's faint, gentle glow,
The heart takes flight, but the mind moves slow.
Feelings swirl, a tempest inside,
Yet the language of love tends to hide.

Fingers trace paths on the fabric of night,
Hoping to spark a flicker of light.
Each glance exchanged, a story untold,
In the spaces between, the truth must unfold.

So here in the hush, where shadows abide,
A dance of the inarticulate, they bide.
With every breath, a promise unspun,
In the stillness, their journey's begun.

The Weight of Untold Stories

In the corners of my mind,
Whispers echo, soft yet clear.
Secrets wrapped in silence tight,
Yearning for a voice to hear.

Each tale woven in the dark,
Fingers trace a fragile line.
Moments lost, but still they spark,
Waiting for the sun to shine.

Heavy hearts carry the load,
Burden borne, yet rarely spoke.
Hidden paths that we have strode,
In each shadow, memories cloak.

A sigh escapes, a breath released,
Words that linger, faint yet bold.
Stories rest, yet never ceased,
In their depths, the truth unfolds.

What tales lie beneath the skin?
The weight of dreams, a heavy crown.
Voices rise as silence thins,
Untold stories wear me down.

Whispers in the Stillness

In the calm of evening's glow,
Softly hums the night's embrace.
Stars above, a silent show,
Listening in a sacred space.

Moonlight dances on the leaves,
Bringing forth a gentle sigh.
Nature's breath, the heart believes,
In the stillness, dreams can fly.

Echoes of a lover's call,
Promises on the evening air.
Everything feels wondrous, small,
In the quiet, hearts lay bare.

Thoughts like shadows drift and flow,
Whispers of the world unseen.
Every secret that we sow,
Grows with dreams that intervene.

Moments linger, soft and sweet,
Cradled gently in the night.
In this stillness, life's heartbeat,
Transforms silence into light.

Shadows of Unexpressed Thoughts

In the corners of the mind,
Shadows dance with silent grace.
Thoughts remain so intertwined,
    Hiding in a vacant space.

Words unsaid, a heavy veil,
Every pause, a silent scream.
In the dark, they softly trail,
Chasing after whispered dreams.

Each expression left unturned,
Burns like embers in the night.
Lessons that we've never learned,
    Fading slowly from our sight.

Secrets dwell where no one sees,
Haunted by the things we fear.
In the echoes, softest pleas,
Speak of what we hold so dear.

In the light, those shadows speak,
    Urging us to break the chain.
Through the silence, voices peak,
    Finding freedom in the pain.

A Symphony in Quietude

Softly plays the world around,
Nature's notes, a gentle song.
In the silence, peace is found,
Where the heart can dream along.

Rustling leaves, a whispered tune,
Echoes drape the evening's light.
Underneath the silver moon,
Moments blend in tranquil flight.

Each heartbeat marks the time we share,
Melodies of love and grace.
In this stillness, souls lay bare,
As the stars begin to trace.

Harmony in every breath,
Life composed in subtle ways.
In the quiet, conquers death,
Stringing dreams through endless days.

From the silence, music grows,
Soft as shadows touch the ground.
In the calm, true beauty flows,
Crafting peace in every sound.

Unspilled Ink

In shadows deep, the thoughts abide,
A silent dance, with naught to hide.
Each word unsaid, a treasure stored,
In pages blank, where dreams are scored.

The quill awaits, for dreams to flow,
Yet fear stays close, a heavy glow.
Unspilled ink lies in wait for fate,
A symphony of words to create.

With every stroke, a whisper grows,
Though no one hears, the heart still knows.
In written silence, secrets dwell,
In unspilled ink, all tales compel.

A canvas vast, yet wordless still,
Each silent scream, a yearning will.
To craft a world from thoughts confined,
In unspilled ink, our souls aligned.

The ink may sit on pages white,
Yet in the heart, it glows so bright.
So let it flow, release the sound,
In unspilled ink, our love is found.

The Inarticulate Heart

In quiet corners of my mind,
A voice resides, yet hard to find.
It beats a rhythm, strong and true,
But words elude, like morning dew.

This heart, it sings through sighs and tears,
An inarticulate song through years.
With every pulse, a tale untold,
In silent whispers, love takes hold.

It longs for touch, a hand to clasp,
In frozen words, it cannot grasp.
Yet in its depths, rich colors swirl,
A canvas bright, a hidden pearl.

The silence speaks in echoes loud,
In crowded rooms, yet feeling proud.
For inarticulate hearts still soar,
With love profound, forevermore.

So let them beat, in muted grace,
These hidden hearts, they leave a trace.
Beyond the words we think to share,
The inarticulate hearts still care.

Whispered Longing

In shadows cast, a breath escapes,
A whispered longing, hope reshapes.
With every sigh, a story weaves,
In twilight's glow, my heart believes.

The stars align, as dreams ignite,
In quiet places, love takes flight.
Each lingering glance, a silent plea,
In whispered longing, we are free.

Through gentle winds, your name I call,
A soft embrace, a sweet enthrall.
In secret spaces, our souls entwined,
Whispered longings, perfectly aligned.

With every heartbeat, distance fades,
In whispered tones, the night cascades.
A melody sung, just out of sight,
In whispered longing, all feels right.

So let the night bear witness true,
To whispered longings, me and you.
In every secret, we reside,
Whispered longings, hearts collide.

The Unseen Dialogue

Two souls that meet yet words are few,
An unseen dialogue, me and you.
In fleeting glances, stories blend,
In silence shared, hearts transcend.

The eyes converse, a gentle glance,
In every moment, a silent dance.
Though lips are sealed, emotions flow,
In an unseen dialogue, love does grow.

With every breath, a language new,
In shared stillness, feelings brew.
The heart knows well what words can't say,
In unseen dialogue, we find our way.

Each heartbeat sings, a secret song,
In whispered thoughts, where we belong.
A bond unbroken, firm and true,
In unseen dialogue, me and you.

So let the world around us fade,
In this communion, unafraid.
For in the silence, love can thrive,
In unseen dialogues, we arrive.

Unseen Horizons of Emotion

In the quiet depths we hide,
Whispers linger just outside.
Shadows dance on fragile walls,
Echoes fill the empty halls.

Fear and hope begin to blend,
On this journey without end.
Silent tears, a stormy sky,
Holding dreams that drift and fly.

Every heartbeat weaves a thread,
Path untaken, words unsaid.
In the silence, hearts still beat,
Searching for that rare retreat.

Memories fade like distant stars,
Scars remind us of our scars.
Yet through darkness, light will break,
softly guiding, never fake.

As we gaze beyond the veil,
Finding strength in love's soft trail.
Unseen horizons call our name,
In this dance, we play the game.

The Language We Never Spoke

Words unsaid hang in the air,
Secrets linger, hearts laid bare.
In the silence, feelings grow,
Yearning flames yet to bestow.

Eyes converse, a tender trace,
Mapping thoughts on a shared space.
Silent laughter paints the night,
In the darkness, love takes flight.

Fingers brush, electric spark,
In our hearts, we leave a mark.
No need for sound to convey,
What deep emotions long to say.

Dreams entwined like vines in spring,
Boundless hopes that always cling.
In this quiet, souls combine,
Crafting verses, hearts align.

Though we lack the words to share,
In each glance, we find our prayer.
A hidden bond that grows and speaks,
Love's true language, soft and meek.

The Nocturne of Unarticulated Wishes

In twilight's hush, desires bloom,
Silent cries break through the gloom.
Each unvoiced wish, a gentle sigh,
Floating softly, nowhere to lie.

Moonlit paths hold echoes near,
Fragrant dreams that disappear.
In the dark, they twist and weave,
Leaving traces, hard to believe.

Stars above, the night's embrace,
Whisper secrets, time and space.
In shadows deep, hopes take their flight,
Guided by the tender night.

Melodies that no one hears,
Intertwined with muted fears.
Yet in silence, wishes swell,
Carried forth, a wishful spell.

As dawn breaks, they fade away,
Unforgettable, yet they stay.
In the dreamscape, we still chase,
Nocturne's haunting, endless grace.

Unfamiliar Cadences

In rhythms strange, we find our way,
Hearts in sync, yet far astray.
Notes entwined, a symphony,
Lost in between, you and me.

Each moment plays a different tune,
A melody beneath the moon.
Fingers touch, a fleeting sound,
In this dance, our souls are bound.

Language formed of breath and sighs,
Unfamiliar but never lies.
Harmonies that clash and blend,
In this journey, hearts transcend.

Chasing echoes through the night,
Seeking out that distant light.
Though we stumble on this path,
Together we embrace the wrath.

Through the chaos, love remains,
Unspoken laughter, silent pains.
Cadences that softly call,
In this rhythm, we stand tall.

Sheltered Thoughts

In the quiet of the night,
Whispers dance on moonlit ground.
Thoughts like shadows take their flight,
In solitude, my heart is found.

Cradled dreams in gentle hands,
Fleeting moments, soft and light.
Through the dark, the spirit stands,
Embracing peace until the bright.

Wrapped in warmth, where stillness sits,
I trace the outlines of my fears.
In every pause, my mind admits,
The shelter formed from silent tears.

Thoughts retreat, then intertwine,
In corners where the heart can play.
In gentle breaths, I seek the sign,
Of tomorrows yet to sway.

A haven built on fleeting sighs,
Here I dwell, away from strife.
Beneath the stars, my spirit flies,
In this shelter, I find life.

The Unspoken Bond

In a gaze, a secret shared,
Words unspoken, yet so clear.
Feelings linger, hearts laid bare,
In silence formed, we draw near.

Hands brushed softly, sparks ignite,
Time suspends in quiet grace.
In each moment, pure delight,
A bond that time cannot erase.

Life unfolds in whispered tones,
Echoes pulse beneath the skin.
Between the lines, our heartbeats drone,
In every loss, we still can win.

Through every trial, we remain,
A duo forged in love's embrace.
In joy and sorrow, we contain,
The magic found in our own space.

Though words may fail, the truth is known,
In every glance, we hold the key.
In tenderness, our love has grown,
In silence, we are truly free.

Lingering Silences

In moments when the world holds still,
Breath catches on a fading breeze.
Silence hums, a subtle thrill,
In stillness, time begins to freeze.

Each heartbeat echoes in the dark,
An unvoiced song of deep connection.
In the quiet, kindred sparks,
Ignite a tender recollection.

Words may falter, but souls align,
In uncharted paths, we find.
Each lingering silence is a sign,
That speaks the language of the mind.

As shadows stretch and day takes flight,
We share the weight of unmade dreams.
In every pause, we hold the light,
Of hopes that shimmer, or so it seems.

The echoes of our heartbeats chase,
The emptiness that silence brings.
In fleeting glances, we embrace,
The bond that lives in whispered wings.

Echoing Feelings

In the chambers of my heart,
Feelings ripple, soft and deep.
Waves of joy and sorrow part,
In moonlit nights, I find my keep.

With every thought, a story flows,
Resonating through the years.
Echoes linger, ebbing lows,
In silence held, the heart appears.

Fleeting moments etched in time,
Chasing shadows, chasing light.
In each pulse, a quiet rhyme,
That dances softly through the night.

Through the beauty and the pain,
We capture fragments, piece by piece.
In this echo, love remains,
A tapestry of sweet release.

In the stillness, truth reveals,
The depth of all we dare to feel.
In echoes vast, our spirit heals,
As love surrounds us, ever real.

Between the Lines of Silence

In hushed corners, whispers dwell,
Echoes of stories we dare not tell.
Shadows dance in muted light,
Words linger softly, just out of sight.

Through quiet breaths, we seek to find,
The truths concealed, the ties that bind.
In the pauses, secrets bloom,
Between the lines, we sense the loom.

A fragile thread connects our fate,
In silence, we learn to wait.
With every heartbeat, tales unwind,
Between the lines, love's notes remind.

So let us pause and listen deep,
Where silence stirs, and dreams still creep.
In unseen spaces, hear the call,
Between the lines, we rise and fall.

The Murmurs of What Remains

A whisper drifts on evening air,
Among the ruins, memories stare.
Footsteps echo on paths once free,
In softest tones, they call to me.

What lingers now, unseen yet clear,
The tales of yesteryear draw near.
With every sigh, a tale unfolds,
In murmurs soft, my heart enfolds.

Beneath the stars, a canvas bare,
We paint with shadows, rich and rare.
The silent songs of what's been lost,
In quiet hope, we bear the cost.

Yet in the silence, spirits rise,
With every tear, the past complies.
In gentle hands, I hold the thread,
The murmurs guide where dreams are led.

A Tapestry of Untold Paths

Threads of color weave and twine,
In every cross, a chance to shine.
Paths diverge and then align,
A tapestry, by fate's design.

Stories hidden, yearning for light,
In whispers soft, they take to flight.
Each journey laced with hope and fear,
In tangled knots, the heart draws near.

Forgotten dreams lie intertwined,
In every stitch, echoes remind.
Worn hands work where shadows blend,
A tapestry that knows no end.

Life's rich fabric, worn yet bold,
In strands of silver and threads of gold.
With every knot, a memory's spark,
A tapestry sewn in the dark.

Secrets Woven in Stillness

In quietude, the heart reveals,
The place where silence softly heals.
Beneath the calm, a story thrums,
In hidden depths, a spirit hums.

The stillness breathes, it knows my name,
In shadows' grasp, I find my aim.
Secrets rest where few will tread,
In woven threads, the paths I've fled.

As time unwinds, the moments blend,
In stillness waits, the truth, my friend.
I gather whispers, soft and light,
Secrets woven in the night.

Each breath a treasure, each moment rare,
In stillness, I find the love I share.
Embracing all, the past in sight,
In woven stillness, I seek the light.

The Canvas of Unspoken Emotions

Brush strokes hide the secrets told,
In colors, vibrant, vivid, bold.
Each hue a whisper, soft and shy,
An art of feelings passing by.

With every shade, a story grows,
Layered depths, nobody knows.
The silence speaks, the canvas sighs,
In gentle strokes, the heart complies.

Dreams woven in a tapestry bright,
Chasing shadows, seeking light.
The palette flips, emotions swirl,
In every stroke, a hidden pearl.

The easel stands, a bold embrace,
A sacred trust in this space.
Beyond the view, the soul must roam,
In painted echoes, we find home.

Hidden Chords of the Heart

In silence, melodies reside,
Strummed softly where secrets hide.
A heartbeat's rhythm, a quiet tune,
Underneath the watchful moon.

Strings of fate weave through the air,
Chords that linger, light as prayer.
Harmonies that dance and play,
Invisible notes, shaping the day.

When solitude swells like a tide,
Those hidden chords cannot bide.
They rise and fall, as whispers blend,
A gentle touch, a soothing friend.

In the echoes, love's refrain,
Cradled soft in joy and pain.
Each strum a promise, a spark divine,
In heart's composition, a sweet design.

Unwritten Chapters of Connection

Pages blank, we forge ahead,
In spaces where the words are bred.
With every glance, we turn the key,
Unlocking what is meant to be.

Our stories blend, and silence speaks,
In subtle ways, our heart still seeks.
Each chapter starts with trust anew,
In lines where love shines through.

The ink may fade but feelings last,
Footprints carved in shadows cast.
As seasons shift and stories grow,
In unwritten truth, our hearts will flow.

Together bound, through day and night,
These chapters hold our shared delight.
In every pause, a tale unfolds,
In written whispers, love retold.

The Quiet Between Us

In moments shared with gentle grace,
The quiet weaves a tender space.
No words are needed, just a glance,
In silence, we find our dance.

The softest breath, a language speaks,
In every pause, our spirit seeks.
An understanding, rich and deep,
In stillness, promises we keep.

Time slows down, the world awakes,
In hushed tones, connection makes.
Between our hearts, a bloom of trust,
In every hush, a must.

Together here, in quiet bliss,
A sacred bond, a tender kiss.
The quiet holds what words can't share,
In silent love, a breath of air.

The Louder Quiet

In the stillness, whispers bloom,
Echoes dance in a room.
Thoughts collide, softly tread,
While silence sings what's unsaid.

Moonlight filters through the glass,
Embracing night as moments pass.
Shadows play their gentle games,
In quietude, we find our names.

Every breath, a secret shared,
In this stillness, none are scared.
Voices linger, weave and flow,
In the echoes, we can grow.

Time dissolves in softest hum,
Here in this space, we become.
Loudest truths are softly found,
In the peace where hearts abound.

Listen close, the quiet's plea,
In the hush, we learn to see.
Beneath the noise, the essence lies,
In the quieter, wiser sighs.

Gestures of the Soul

A glance can say what words can't write,
In the silence, souls take flight.
A gentle touch, a subtle sign,
Bridges built, our hearts align.

In every smile, a story shared,
Lives entwined, the hearts are dared.
Fingers brush like autumn leaves,
In these moments, love believes.

Warmth of hands in worn embrace,
Barefoot dances, a tender grace.
Each gesture, a language of its own,
In the quiet, seeds are sown.

Eyes that linger, a sacred space,
In these depths, we find our place.
Not in words, but in the flow,
Of gestures kind, our spirits glow.

Listen to the heart's soft plea,
In every gesture, set it free.
Trust in rhythms, the soul's decree,
In silent love, we find our key.

Beneath the Tongue

Words are treasures, yet to find,
Guarded secrets, tightly bind.
Beneath the tongue, the truth does hide,
In whispered dreams, hearts will bide.

Tales untold in quiet rage,
Chapters lost on life's vast page.
Ink and paper, silent cries,
In the unsaid, wisdom lies.

In the stillness, thoughts ignite,
Shadowed echoes, soft and bright.
Every pause holds deep intent,
In the silence, we're content.

To speak the heart is to lay bare,
Every longing, every care.
Yet, in the hush, we find our song,
In what remains, we still belong.

Listen closely, the words await,
To break the chains, to shift the fate.
Beneath the tongue, the spirit sings,
In every silence, healing brings.

Conversations in Shadows

In twilight's embrace, secrets weave,
Whispers drift where we believe.
Shadows dance in playful light,
Conversations spark the night.

Voices silhouette the moon,
Echoing a gentle tune.
Two souls meet in fading glow,
Where the unspoken seeds do grow.

In the corners of the mind,
Traces of the past we find.
Fragrant memories linger near,
In these shadows, we hold dear.

With every step, the night reveals,
Paths of joy, the heart it heals.
In silence shared, we feel complete,
In shadowed corners, life's heartbeat.

Listen close, the night implores,
In whispered dreams, we open doors.
In conversations, shadows dance,
Where the magic finds its chance.

The Art of Untold Stories

In shadows dark, the whispers dwell,
Words unspoken, hearts to tell.
A canvas blank, with colors bright,
Stories waiting to find their light.

Time weaves magic, soft and slow,
Echoes linger, feelings grow.
Pages turn, the ink will spill,
Crafting tales that breathe and thrill.

Voices merge in silent chime,
Memories dance, defying time.
Each thread woven, a bond so tight,
In this tapestry, lost in light.

Mysterious paths, a journey starts,
In every line, two beating hearts.
Unfolding dreams like ancient scrolls,
The art of stories fills our souls.

So let the ink flow, let it sing,
In every closure, the hope we bring.
For in the silence, truth is found,
The art of stories knows no bound.

Hidden Verses

In quiet corners, secrets hide,
Words unnoticed, deep inside.
A heart's refrain, a whispered tune,
Hidden verses beneath the moon.

Every sigh, a line unspun,
In the silence, two become one.
Beneath the surface, feelings bloom,
Hidden verses find their room.

In shadows cast by dreams once shared,
Vows unspoken, love declared.
Like petals soft, they gently break,
In every pause, the truth we wake.

A book of moments, torn and frayed,
Where every heartbeat's unafraid.
The ink of life writes on each page,
Hidden verses, a timeless sage.

So listen close to what you feel,
For hidden verses often heal.
In quiet places, echoes ring,
The beauty lies in what we bring.

Notes from the Invisible

A whisper soft, it floats away,
In perfect silence, dreams will play.
The unseen notes, they pulse and soar,
A symphony from the evermore.

In shadows deep, the spirits dance,
Unheard melodies, a fleeting glance.
With every heartbeat, a story spins,
In invisible realms, our journey begins.

The air is thick with unsung dreams,
In every silence, a truth redeems.
A gentle breeze carries the sound,
Of notes invisible, all around.

So let your heart be a vibrant drum,
Concealed harmonies, they will come.
In quiet moments, find your grace,
Notes from the invisible leave their trace.

With eyes wide open, see the light,
In shadowed corners, the stars ignite.
For in the unseen, wonders dwell,
Notes from the invisible, a spell.

Unheard Melodies

In twilight's hush, the music sighs,
Unheard melodies beneath the skies.
A symphony in silence found,
In every heartbeat, a subtle sound.

The wind carries whispers, soft and low,
In the stillness, where shadows grow.
Hushed tones flutter like birds in flight,
Unheard melodies dance through the night.

Each note a secret, each pause a breath,
In the quiet, we learn of death.
Life's cadence flows, an ebb and flow,
Unheard melodies, a gentle glow.

Strings of the heart, they gently play,
Crafting symphonies from day to day.
In the silence, we find our song,
Unheard melodies, where we belong.

So close your eyes and listen deep,
In the stillness, the dreams we'll keep.
For in every heart, the music swells,
In unheard melodies, magic dwells.

Cryptic Desires

In shadows deep, wishes sigh,
Whispers linger, dreams awry.
A longing glance, a hidden spark,
Hear the echoes in the dark.

Veils of silence gently sway,
Chasing thoughts that drift away.
Hearts entwined in secret nights,
Craving warmth, elusive lights.

Behind closed doors, the tension grows,
What the heart may never show.
In every pause, a chance awaits,
To speak the words that fate creates.

Fingers brush, electric streams,
Lost in labyrinths of dreams.
A stolen moment, soft and rare,
Time suspends, we're unaware.

Yet cryptic paths lead to the flame,
In whispered truths, we find our name.
Concealed desires, so profound,
In silence, our love's unbound.

Hushed Reveries

Beneath the stars, we find our peace,
In quiet thoughts, the world's release.
Softly spoken, dreams take flight,
In the embrace of velvet night.

Hushed reveries, softly spun,
In fleeting moments, we are one.
Eyes closed tight, hearts open wide,
In the silence, we confide.

Breathing in the night's sweet song,
In stillness where we both belong.
A gentle sigh, a lingering gaze,
In every second, love's pure haze.

The hush of night, a soothing balm,
In the chaos, we find calm.
With every heartbeat, time stands still,
In cherished dreams, we find our will.

Our whispers waltz among the stars,
In hidden truths and healing scars.
Through hushed moments, we unveil,
A love that echoes, yet elusive trail.

Murmurs of the Heart

In silent rooms, feelings bloom,
Soft murmurs chase away the gloom.
A heartbeat shared, a fleeting touch,
In every moment, we feel so much.

Whispers linger, secrets tread,
In the spaces where words are said.
Gentle beats, like distant drums,
In harmony, our longing hums.

Eyes meet softly, time stands still,
In every glance, a warming thrill.
Murmurs of love, beneath the skin,
A quiet strength that draws us in.

Between the lines, we find our way,
In hushed confessions, night and day.
A language born of soul and mind,
In whispered dreams, our paths aligned.

For every secret, a story lives,
In murmurs shared, the heart forgives.
In silken threads, we weave our fate,
Through love's embrace, we resonate.

Unarticulated Truths

In the stillness, truth resides,
Unspoken words our heart confides.
We navigate through space and time,
In unarticulated rhyme.

Barely spoken, they dance around,
In shadows cast, we've always found.
A fragile heart hides what it feels,
Layers deep in love's sealed reels.

Glances stolen, moments missed,
In quiet chaos, love persists.
The weight of thoughts that linger near,
In unarticulated fears.

Between the lines, we seek to tell,
In every silence, love compels.
Through whispered hopes, we carve a way,
To light the dark, to seize the day.

Yet truth remains a mystic dance,
In every smile, an aching chance.
In unarticulated grace, we soar,
Together bound, forevermore.

Secrets in Stillness

In whispers soft the shadows creep,
Where dreams reside and secrets keep.
The silent breath of evening's sigh,
Holds tales beneath the starlit sky.

In corners dark, where echoes blend,
The quietude becomes a friend.
With every pause, the heart takes flight,
In stillness found, the soul ignites.

Among the trees, the whispers weave,
Nature's grace, hard to believe.
A tranquil mind in starry night,
Finds solace in the absence of light.

Time wanders slow, a gentle glide,
As thoughts emerge, like waves, a tide.
In solitude, the truth unfolds,
In secrets shared, a heart consoled.

Let stillness speak, and let it show,
The beauty held in subtle glow.
For in the quiet, life unveils,
The deepest truths that time regales.

The Silence Between Us

A silence hangs, a heavy mist,
Where words should flow, a fragile tryst.
With every glance, a story stalled,
In quiet nights where shadows called.

Your eyes hold worlds I long to see,
Yet here we are, in harmony.
A breath, a pause, and then the stir,
Of thoughts unspoken, heartbeats blur.

In laughter shared, the echoes fade,
Yet threads connect, though silence made.
A bridge of feelings built in trust,
In every pause, a moment's must.

The space between, a canvas wide,
Where unvoiced thoughts and dreams can hide.
An unseen dance, a silent song,
In simplicity, where we belong.

So linger here, let silence play,
In whispered tones, we find our way.
For in this hush, our souls align,
In tender quiet, you are mine.

Shadows of Expression

In corners cast by low-lit beams,
The shadows dance with whispered dreams.
A flicker here, a whisper there,
In twilight's glow, emotions flare.

The canvas speaks in colors bright,
Yet shadows linger, shy from light.
In every stroke, a story hides,
Where fears and hopes, in silence, bide.

The brush it glides, a tender touch,
With every moment holding much.
Yet in the dark, what truths are found?
In shadows deep, our hearts resound.

To speak in forms the mind can't name,
In quiet hues, we play the game.
The shadows sketch what words can't frame,
A dance of thoughts that forge the same.

In every shadow, a tale to tell,
Of unvoiced feelings and the swell.
So let the light and dark combine,
In shadows' grace, our truths entwine.

Lingering Thoughts

Like autumn leaves in crisp, cool air,
Lingering thoughts, a soft despair.
They drift and swirl, then settle slow,
In quiet minds where feelings grow.

What once was clear, now fades away,
Yet echoes linger, here to stay.
A whispered thought, a fleeting glance,
In quiet moments, hearts advance.

The clock ticks on, the world spins round,
Yet in our minds, lost thoughts are found.
They dance like shadows on the wall,
In soft embrace, we rise, we fall.

The weight of dreams, the light of day,
The thoughts that weave, then slip away.
A tapestry of mind's design,
Where echoes wane, yet always shine.

So hold them close, these fleeting shades,
In quiet hours, the heart cascades.
For lingering thoughts are never lost,
They shape our lives, no matter the cost.

The Unexpressed Love Song

In shadows deep, the heart would sigh,
Whispers lost to the night sky.
A melody soft, yet undefined,
Longing notes that intertwine.

Eyes speak words that lips won't dare,
Every glance a secret prayer.
A dance of souls, a silent fight,
Chasing stars in the quiet night.

Time stands still, yet moments flee,
A love confined, a mystery.
In silence blooms a fragrant rose,
Where no one goes, but the heart knows.

Unseen colors paint the air,
In dreams where truths are laid bare.
Each heartbeat resonates with grace,
A love song lost in empty space.

With every breath, we hold it close,
This unexpressed love, we chose.
In secret hours, it shines bright,
A hidden flame igniting the night.

Unsung Tales

In the quiet corners of the mind,
Lies a treasure many won't find.
Stories whispered in the breeze,
Tales of hope that never cease.

Forgotten heroes, their journeys vast,
Moments woven, shadows cast.
Each silent voice, a world untold,
In every heart, a dream of gold.

Rivers flow with memories rare,
From mountains high to valleys bare.
Every step a quiet grace,
In the dance of time and space.

Beneath the stars, their truths reside,
A tapestry where dreams abide.
Unsung tales, they call and weave,
In the night, we dare believe.

The echo of a laugh, a sigh,
Moments captured, drifting by.
In silent realms where whispers stay,
Each unsung tale helps light the way.

Silenced Dreams

In the hush of dawn, they fade away,
Like shadows lost at the break of day.
Dreams unspoken, tucked in deep,
A quiet longing that we keep.

Behind each smile, a wish concealed,
In the heart's chamber, love revealed.
Fading echoes, memories call,
In the silence, we rise and fall.

Threads of hope, they intertwine,
Under the surface, souls align.
In the stillness, they softly cling,
Yearning for the light to bring.

With every heartbeat, whispers soar,
In the void, we seek for more.
Silenced dreams, they yearn to speak,
In the night, we find the weak.

Yet in the silence, a spark ignites,
A dance of shadows, hidden lights.
In the quiet, their echoes play,
Silenced dreams will find the way.

The Unvoiced Journey

Across the sands of time's embrace,
We wander on, a silent chase.
Steps unmarked on life's vast shore,
An unvoiced journey, evermore.

Voices lost in the ambient sound,
In life's chorus, truths abound.
Every heartbeat, a tale unfolds,
As we traverse the paths of old.

In the shadows, we search for light,
On winding roads that veer from sight.
With every twist, a lesson learned,
In the silence, our lights are burned.

Mountains high, and valleys low,
Each step we take helps us grow.
The roads untraveled, they call our name,
In the vast unknown, we stake our claim.

Through every silence, our hopes arise,
In the stillness, we touch the skies.
The unvoiced journey, ever grand,
A path of whispers, hand in hand.

Whispered Hopes

In the shadows where dreams linger,
Softly spoken words take flight,
Carried on the breeze of wishes,
Cradled in the calm of night.

Faintly heard by those who listen,
Echoes of a heart's desire,
Turning whispers into visions,
Igniting an unyielding fire.

Stars above, they gently glisten,
Guiding paths yet to unfold,
In the silence, hope persists,
A promise waiting to be told.

As time flows like a river,
Carving futures in its wake,
Every drop a hidden treasure,
Every ripple, choices make.

Trust the murmurs that are given,
For in quietude they grow,
Out of sight, but ever present,
Whispered hopes that gently glow.

The Silence of Yearning

Beneath the moon's soft silver glow,
Hearts ache in the still of night,
Yearning for a touch unspoken,
Longing for what feels so right.

Quiet moments hold the secrets,
Stored deep in each silent sigh,
Words unvoiced hang in the air,
Filling spaces where dreams lie.

Every glance is filled with meaning,
Every heartbeat feels the strain,
In the hush, love's song is played,
A melody of sweet refrain.

Time stretches in the shadows,
As hope dances on the breeze,
In this silence, souls entwine,
Finding solace, finding peace.

Yet the echoes of desire,
Bound by chains of unspoken dreams,
Draw us close as we can't speak,
In the silence, love redeems.

Shades of the Voiceless

In corners where the shadows play,
Colors blend without a sound,
Voiceless tales begin to weave,
In the silence, dreams are found.

Secrets held in quiet spaces,
Shades that shimmer, fade, and glow,
Each hue whispers untold stories,
From the hearts we seldom show.

Silent battles, wounds concealed,
Mark the canvas of our hearts,
Each stroke tells of struggles fought,
In shadows, hidden beauty starts.

As daylight breaks, the colors flow,
Giving life to what we hide,
The shades of pain and joy collide,
Telling tales we choose to bide.

In every silence, hear the call,
A chorus of the unseen soul,
Where the voiceless find their power,
In their depths, we become whole.

The Beauty of the Unsaid

Between the lines of quiet papers,
Lies a world of golden dreams,
Where words remain softly nameless,
Yet they glow in silken seams.

In the pauses, we find meaning,
In the spaces, love resides,
Language lost in gentle glances,
A truth that time merely hides.

Moments passed with hearts unspoken,
Craft their own unique tale,
In the beauty of the unsaid,
Feelings travel without fail.

Each heartbeat speaks in silence,
Echoes through the air we share,
In what's not said, lies our freedom,
In unspoken, we declare.

Love often dances in the stillness,
In the shadows of the mind,
The beauty of what we don't voice,
Is the treasure we may find.

Silent Symphonies of the Soul

In the hush of twilight's glow,
Whispers of dreams begin to flow.
Notes of longing fill the air,
Carried gently on the prayer.

Strings of silence, softly played,
In heart's chambers, serenade.
Melodies of what we feel,
Unraveled truths that time reveals.

Echoes dance on breeze's wings,
Tales of love and fragile things.
Notes composed in quiet nights,
Search for warmth in fleeting lights.

Fragrant hope on softest sighs,
Awakens worlds beneath the skies.
In every pause, a song unfolds,
A symphony in silence molds.

In the stillness, feelings bloom,
A boundless heart, a vastened room.
Harmonies of light and shade,
The soul's music, unafraid.

The Space Between Heartbeats

In the stillness, time holds breath,
Moments frozen, shadows met.
Between each pulse, a story lies,
Whispers echo, soft reply.

When silence stretches, stretched like strings,
In that gap, our longing sings.
A heartbeat's pause, a chance to feel,
The depth of dreams, the truth revealed.

Tender echoes rise and fall,
In the hushed, we heed its call.
Shadows lingering, thoughts collide,
In every pause, love's secrets bide.

Bated breath, the quiet speaks,
A language born of soft mystique.
In this void, we find our way,
Guided by the heart's ballet.

A rhythm forged in silent grace,
In quietude, we find our place.
The space between, a sacred thread,
Woven by all that's left unsaid.

Echoes of the Unsaid

In the dark, emotions bloom,
Words untold hide in the gloom.
Silken threads of thoughts profound,
Resonate with silent sound.

Unvoiced dreams linger in air,
Carried softly, everywhere.
Between the lines, a truth may lie,
A whispered wish, a fleeting sigh.

In every glance, a story waits,
Lost in the dance of fate's debates.
Hidden meanings, veiled and shy,
Like stars withdrawn from the sky.

Unspoken love in shadows hides,
Rides the current where time bides.
Yet in silence, we can find,
The deepest ties that bind mankind.

In the void, reflections spark,
A gentle light against the dark.
Echoes linger, soft and true,
In the gaps, the heart breaks through.

Invisible Ink of Feelings

On paper white, emotions bleed,
Words unwritten, souls indeed.
Ink of feelings, unseen grace,
Reveals the heart's concealed embrace.

In every stroke, a tear may fall,
The essence captured, one and all.
Echoes live in margins bare,
A canvas filled with love and care.

Scribbled thoughts, in shadows dwell,
In the silence, words compel.
Lines unwound, a tender trace,
Invisible ink, every space.

What is spoken, what is sought,
In the folds, the lessons taught.
Like whispers penned, forever craved,
Unseen threads, the heart is braved.

The beauty lies in what we feel,
True stories crafted, finely real.
Invisible lore in life's ink spun,
A tapestry of hearts in one.

The Space Between Words

In whispers soft, the silence grows,
Where every thought, with caution, flows.
The weight of hopes, the fear it brings,
In quiet breaths, the essence sings.

A pause where meaning often hides,
The distance felt, where silence bides.
The longing stirs, an unseen thread,
Connecting souls, though words unsaid.

In shadows cast by fleeting light,
Two hearts can dance in endless night.
With every glance, a story told,
In silence deep, their love unfolds.

The gap expands, yet draws us near,
A tender bond that's crystal clear.
The space between, a sacred place,
Where every heartbeat leaves a trace.

So let us dwell in this embrace,
In quietude, we find our grace.
Though words may falter, we can see,
In silence, love will always be.

Cryptic Echoes

In corridors of time we roam,
Where echoes whisper, lost from home.
Each sound a secret yet untold,
In shadows dark, the past unfolds.

The fleeting trails of days gone by,
In whispered tales, the reasons why.
With every step, a ghostly sigh,
As memories linger, never die.

Through curtains worn by light and age,
We turn the key, unlock the cage.
The cryptic clues in laughter's ring,
Resonant notes that softly sing.

In faded letters, lines once bright,
Become the dusk, transform the light.
Yet every echo has its place,
A haunting tune, a soft embrace.

So listen close and keep it near,
The whispers of what once was clear.
In cryptic echoes, truth will gleam,
As past and present weave a dream.

Unrecorded Moments

In fleeting seconds, time escapes,
A treasure trove of silent shapes.
The laughter shared, the quiet sighs,
Are written deep within our eyes.

Beneath the stars, in twilight's glow,
We live through days that come and go.
The brush of hands, a fleeting spark,
The unrecorded lights the dark.

In gentle whispers, secrets shared,
The warmth conveyed, the love declared.
Each heartbeat feels like poetry,
In moments lost, yet meant to be.

As time rolls on, we find our way,
Through paths untraveled, night and day.
In every glance, we steal the time,
Creating worlds, eternally sublime.

So hold these moments, soft and frail,
In memories where dreams set sail.
Though unrecorded, they're not in vain,
In every heartbeat, love remains.

Lingual Emptiness

In words unspoken, gaps appear,
A void where meaning hides in fear.
The silence fills the air we breathe,
In lingual stretches, hearts believe.

With every language, walls we build,
Yet still, the silence can be filled.
An echo of thoughts, a missing thread,
Where conversations go unfed.

The struggle found in voicing truth,
The ache of longing, lost in youth.
In pauses deep, we find our way,
Through lingual emptiness, we sway.

The space between each phrase we crave,
Holds all the things we wish to save.
In absence, we find something real,
A language made of how we feel.

So let the silence intertwine,
With every heartbeat, make it shine.
In lingual emptiness, embrace,
The love that lingers, time can't erase.

Feelings Left Behind

In shadows where whispers dwell,
Memories echo, weaving a spell.
Unspoken words, a heavy load,
Carried alone on this weary road.

Time folds softly, like a fading dream,
Silent tears in a restless stream.
Each heartbeat marks a ghostly trace,
Of laughter lost in an empty space.

Like footprints washed from sandy shores,
The heart recalls what it ignores.
Yet in the silence, hope still glows,
Like a tender bud, where longing grows.

What once was bright is now a shade,
Yet in the twilight, love won't fade.
With every sigh, a flicker shines,
In the garden where loss entwines.

Though feelings linger, shadows wane,
In letting go, there's still a gain.
For in each heart, a seed can find,
The strength to bloom, though left behind.

Silent Interludes

Inbetween breaths, the world stands still,
Echoes hush, as time begins to thrill.
Moments pause, wrapped in gentle grace,
As silence unfolds in a sacred space.

Notes unplayed linger in the air,
Unseen melodies, soft as a prayer.
A heartbeat sways to an unstrung song,
In the stillness, we somehow belong.

Eyes meet softly, whispers unheard,
Thoughts unspoken, like a hidden bird.
Each glance a story, a thread unwinds,
In the tapestry of intertwined minds.

Little pauses in the daily rush,
Where solitude offers a calming hush.
In the quiet, hearts can align,
Finding solace in the subtle sign.

Moments treasured, as shadows blend,
In silent interludes, we transcend.
For in these stillness, life feels wide,
Wrapping us gently, as time collides.

Unshared Journeys

Paths diverge under starlit night,
Dreams take flight, hidden from sight.
Wanderers roam, each on their own,
In the quiet stars, the seeds are sown.

With every step, stories unfold,
Adventures whispered, yet never told.
Each tale a treasure, lost in the mist,
Unseen journeys in the hearts of the brisk.

On winding roads, we search for peace,
Finding beauty in the bits that cease.
Voices carried by the wind's soft sigh,
A chorus of hopes that neither die.

As travelers part, we hold the flame,
Of moments shared without a name.
In solitude's grace, we learn to dance,
In the spaces where life offers a chance.

Though paths may stray and distances grow,
In unshared journeys, the spirit flows.
For every footfall marks a sign,
Of the love that binds, through space and time.

Breathless Confessions

In the hush, a secret breathes,
Soft confessions wrapped in leaves.
The heart races, words find tether,
In whispered dreams beneath the weather.

Vulnerable truths spill from the soul,
Every syllable, a fleeting goal.
With trembling lips and gazes locked,
Time suspends as emotions are unlocked.

In quiet moments, courage swells,
Breaking through, like ringing bells.
Every confession carries a weight,
A fragile bond that seals our fate.

With each heartbeat, a story told,
Of fears, of hopes, in silence bold.
The air thickens with things left unsaid,
Yet in these whispers, love is fed.

Breathless confessions that intertwine,
Binding souls in a sacred line.
In the warmth of honesty, we find relief,
In every sigh, a piece of belief.

Veiled Sentiments

In shadows cast by silent thoughts,
Emotions linger, caught in knots.
Whispers fade, like dusk's embrace,
Yearning hearts find no safe place.

Behind the veil, a tale untold,
A canvas painted without bold.
Fragments of dreams, so close yet far,
Echoes of love, like a distant star.

Hidden desires dance in the night,
Fleeting glances, a stolen light.
Moments trapped in a fleeting sigh,
Veiled sentiments that never die.

In silence broken, words unsaid,
The weight of longing fills the bed.
Fingers brush, a fleeting touch,
A reminder of how we feel so much.

Yet still we hold what lies within,
A tapestry woven with light and sin.
For in the shadows love does thrive,
Veiled sentiments keep hope alive.

Relics of Unexpressed Longing

In a chest of memories, dusty and old,
Lie relics of wishes, timid and bold.
Faded love letters, torn and frayed,
Whispers of secrets, quietly laid.

Each item a story, a dream once grand,
Echoes of laughter we once had planned.
But time moved on, like shifting sand,
Leaving behind what we couldn't withstand.

Locked in the shadows, emotions reside,
The depth of our yearning, we chose to hide.
In the silence that lingers, ghosts remain,
Relics of longing, tinged with pain.

A glance across the room, a fleeting chance,
Yet words escape like a wretched dance.
We carry our burdens, old and deep,
In unexpressed longing, we silently weep.

So here in the quiet, the heart takes flight,
Craving the touch, the warmth of the light.
Each relic a whisper that calls to me,
Unexpressed longing, forever free.

Nameless Whispers

In the still of night, nameless whispers flow,
Soft secrets shared where the shadows grow.
Fleeting moments brushed by the dark,
Echoes of feelings, a tender spark.

Words untethered, unspoken truth,
Waves of emotion from the well of youth.
Sighs carry softly, missed by the breeze,
Nameless whispers that never cease.

Glimmers of hope, hidden in sighs,
Reflections of dreams in each other's eyes.
Silent confessions wrap 'round the heart,
Like threads of connection that never depart.

Yet still they linger, these whispers of fate,
Building a bridge where love can await.
In their embrace, the world feels right,
Nameless whispers shaping the night.

With every heartbeat, they gently entwine,
In the dance of longing, so pure and divine.
Voiceless yet vibrant, they endlessly hum,
Nameless whispers, where we are from.

The Unfolding of Untold Truths

In the folds of time, secrets lie still,
Untold truths waiting for courage's thrill.
As petals unfurl in the morning light,
So too do we seek to share our insight.

With trembling hands, we peel back the layers,
Revealing the heart, all its players.
The stories we guard, the pain we conceal,
In the unfolding, we learn to heal.

Silent no longer, we rise from the dark,
Untold truths lighting a passionate spark.
Through trembling breaths, convictions ignite,
In the vulnerability, we find our sight.

Each revelation, a fragile thread,
Woven together in words unsaid.
In this tapestry of shared desire,
The unfolding reveals what we truly aspire.

So step into the light, let shadows release,
Embrace the unknown, find solace and peace.
For in the unveiling, we're finally free,
The unfolding of truths, for you and for me.

Threads of the Unsung

In shadows where whispers reside,
Voices of the unheard abide.
Each note a story, each pause a song,
Weaving a tapestry where dreams belong.

A quiet strength, in the silence laid,
The unsung heroes, never displayed.
Each heartbeat echoes, a pulse of the night,
Bringing forth colors, both subtle and bright.

Tangled in moments that weave and sway,
In the fabric of life, they gently lay.
Invisible threads, yet firm and true,
Binding us all, both me and you.

Through storms unspoken, courage will rise,
Threads of the unsung meet our eyes.
In every soft sorrow, a deep, hidden strength,
Carving our paths, extending our length.

So hold dear the tales that go unheard,
In the silence, let truth be stirred.
For even the quiet find ways to sing,
In the heart's deep chambers, hope takes wing.

In the Gaps of Meaning

Between the lines where stories fade,
Lies a truth that is often delayed.
The spaces that linger, unfilled yet loud,
Whispering secrets beneath the crowd.

In the quietest corners, wisdom looms,
Within the silence, inspiration blooms.
Each pause a question, each breath a plea,
Searching for answers in what's yet to be.

The cracks in our thoughts let the light stream in,
Illuminating shadows, uncovering kin.
In the gaps of meaning, we find our grace,
Embracing the journey, we start to trace.

Words can falter, as feelings collide,
Yet in the silence, we learn to abide.
Through the voids and echoes, a language grows,
In the gaps of meaning, our true self shows.

So let us explore this uncharted space,
Where sense and confusion often embrace.
In every pause, let us seek the true,
The depths of our hearts, waiting on cue.

The Uncharted Terrain of Silence

In the deep where no sound may flow,
Lies a realm that few dare to know.
The silence wraps 'round like a cloak,
Holding secrets that words never spoke.

With each subtle shift, the shadows dance,
In the void, there lies a chance.
Perhaps in the stillness, we find our might,
Navigating the dark, reaching for light.

Maps uncharted, guiding the way,
In echoes of silence, we learn to sway.
Nature's whispers, soft and divine,
Invite us to linger, pause in the line.

Through valleys of quiet, we wander and roam,
Finding solace in the unknown to call home.
In the uncharted, our truths will align,
With each breath of silence, we learn to define.

So step into quiet, let courage take hold,
In the silence, find stories untold.
For in the uncharted, amidst tranquil grace,
We discover our spirit, our own sacred space.

Soliloquies in Solitude

In the hush of one's thoughts, a voice can arise,
Whispers of dreams and the heart's quiet sighs.
A soliloquy echoes, soft yet profound,
In the corners of solitude, wisdom is found.

The silence embraces, a canvas so vast,
Painting the moments that silently pass.
Each word a reflection of what lies within,
In the dance of the stillness, we find where we've been.

Through whispers of longing, we wade through our fears,

In soliloquies woven from laughter and tears.
The songs of our souls weave a tapestry bright,
Illuminating shadows with flickers of light.

In solitude's cradle, we learn to be whole,
Each echo a fragment, a piece of our soul.
Through moments of stillness, we learn to converse,
Crafting our narratives, both blessing and curse.

So savor the silence, let your spirit soar,
In soliloquies sweet, we uncover much more.
For within each reflection, the truth shines so clear,
Embracing the journey, dispelling all fear.

Breath of Unsaid Dreams

In the stillness of the night,
Whispers float on silver light,
Hopes are woven, soft and clear,
Echoes dance, yet disappear.

Stars above begin to gleam,
Carrying every hidden dream,
In the shadows, wishes play,
Finding paths to light their way.

Silent hopes, they mingle fast,
In the future, in the past,
An embrace of what could be,
Unfolding gently, wild and free.

Each breath taken, fleeting tune,
Plays beneath the watchful moon,
Crafting worlds that lie unseen,
In the heart where dreams convene.

So let the night our secrets keep,
In the dark, our visions leap,
Breath of dreams shall never cease,
Finding solace, finding peace.

The Language of the Unspeakable

In silence, truths begin to bloom,
Words unspoken pierce the gloom,
A glance, a sigh, a fleeting pause,
Speak the love without a cause.

Hands that touch like softest rain,
Communicate the hidden pain,
In the quiet, stories flow,
Through every look, the heart will show.

Echoes linger in the air,
Where the mind's eye starts to stare,
A subtle dance of souls entwined,
In the unsaid, a bond defined.

Moments treasured, lost in time,
Whispers soft as distant chime,
The language waits for hearts to choose,
To delve in depths they cannot lose.

So meet me where we dare not speak,
In silence, love, we find the peak,
Unlock the door with tender grace,
In this language, time and space.

Hushed Verses of the Heart

In twilight's embrace, secrets stay,
Softly woven in shades of gray,
Each heartbeat carries a sweet song,
In the quiet, we both belong.

Gentle sighs like whispers flow,
In every pause, a tale to know,
The verses writ in tender flesh,
Reside in silence, deep and fresh.

Eyes that meet, a spark ignites,
Poetry born beneath the lights,
A muted chorus in the night,
Where love's soft shadows take their flight.

Emotions dance like autumn leaves,
Finding solace in what believes,
Each hushed line speaks pure and true,
In the stillness, just me and you.

Let time unfold our sacred art,
In whispered words, we'll never part,
For in this hush, our hearts unite,
In verses soft, our love takes flight.

Pages Left Blank

A journal waits in quiet grace,
Inkless pages, an empty space,
Within these sheets, dreams yet to pen,
Whispers hold a world within.

Blank lines stretch like endless skies,
Craving stories, searching why,
Each hesitant word, a gentle stir,
Awaiting voices, hearts to confer.

Hopeful thoughts dance on the edge,
Yearning to break the silent hedge,
In every gap, a tale concealed,
With promises the heart has sealed.

Time moves on, the ink may dry,
Yet dreams unfurl and take to fly,
In stillness, time writes its song,
Hope lives here, where we belong.

So fill these pages, let it flow,
The words of life, the ebb and glow,
With every stroke, our voices blend,
In each blank space, our lives transcend.

Unheard Echoes

In shadows cast by fading light,
Whispers linger, out of sight.
Footsteps fade on cobbled stone,
Memories etched, yet left alone.

Time's passage marks the silent air,
Voices lost in muted prayer.
Every heartbeat, a ghostly sound,
In the stillness, truths are found.

Reflections dance on twilight's stream,
Caught between the lost and dream.
The echoes call through night's embrace,
Unheard, yet touch the time and space.

Beneath the weight of iron skies,
The heart bears witness, never lies.
Each echo weaves a tale untold,
In silence deep, the brave grow bold.

These unheard echoes softly glide,
Through realm of shadows, far and wide.
Lingering hopes in whispered tones,
A chorus born of silent stones.

The Art of What Remains Unsaid

Words left hanging in the air,
Paint the canvas of despair.
Delicate truths, like fragile glass,
In silence shared, they softly pass.

A glance speaks of a heavy heart,
In quiet moments, worlds depart.
Sighs linger, yet no voice breaks,
In unvoiced thoughts, the soul awakes.

The weight of silence, thick as night,
Holds the promise of hidden light.
Between the lines, emotions flow,
In the unsaid, true feelings grow.

With every pause, our worlds collide,
In uncharted realms where hopes abide.
Conversations fade, yet linger long,
In the spaces where we belong.

What remains unspoken, yet clear,
Crafts a story that draws us near.
Embracing silence, we understand,
The art of life, crafted by hand.

Unvoiced Reveries

In the depth of the quiet night,
Dreams unfurl in muted light.
Thoughts drift softly, like a breeze,
Carrying wishes through the trees.

Unvoiced reveries take their flight,
Painting visions out of sight.
Each heartbeat, a silent song,
In longing whispers, we belong.

Eyes closed tight, the mind awakes,
In secret places, love remakes.
Fleeting shadows, hints of grace,
In tender thoughts, we find our place.

A journey starts where silence reigns,
In hidden paths where hope remains.
The unspoken dreams break through the dark,
To gently weave their subtle spark.

Unvoiced reveries softly sigh,
Painting stars across the sky.
In the hush, our spirits dance,
To dreams unspoken, we take a chance.

The Silence of Forgotten Conversations

Words once shared, now fade away,
In the silence of yesterday.
Faded echoes, soft as dew,
Whispers linger, yet feel so few.

Conversations drift on tired winds,
In the shadows, the heart rescinds.
Once vibrant tales, now mere ghosts,
The silence speaks, our past it boasts.

Time erodes the ink on page,
Yet feelings linger, trapped in cage.
Forgotten moments, bittersweet,
In recalled laughter, shadows meet.

The silence of truths held tight,
Bears witness to the fading light.
Each sigh a prayer, each pause a plea,
In forgotten talks, what used to be.

With every silence, stories wane,
Lost in the dance of joy and pain.
The echo of what once did last,
Is a silent harmony, held fast.

Silent Echoes

In the hush of twilight's grace,
Shadows dance, a silent trace.
Voices linger, soft and low,
Carried whispers, ebb and flow.

Memory's touch, a fleeting gleam,
Fractured light, a broken dream.
Silent echoes, secrets keep,
In the depths where shadows weep.

Time stands still, a pause divine,
In the silence, hearts entwine.
Words unspoken, felt in soul,
Silent echoes make us whole.

Yet beneath the quiet veil,
Stories linger, detail frail.
In the calm, a storm does brew,
Silent echoes, calling you.

Hear the whispers, soft, discreet,
In the silence, feel the beat.
Threads of time, we stitch and sew,
In the silence, love will grow.

Whispers in the Gaps

Between the words, a space appears,
A silent realm, a sea of fears.
In every pause, a meaning lives,
An unspoken truth that softly gives.

Whispers drift like autumn leaves,
Catching breaths in tangled eves.
In the gaps, the heart conveys,
A lullaby of secret ways.

Fingers trace the lines of thought,
In quiet moments, battles fought.
The echoes linger, soft and bare,
Whispers dance upon the air.

Spaces between each lonely sigh,
In those gaps, we learn to fly.
In whispered tones, our souls connect,
Finding solace in the wreck.

Listen close, the world will speak,
In hushed tones, the timid seek.
Whispers in the gaps we find,
A testament to love entwined.

Unsaid Poetry

In the silence, verses bloom,
Thoughts retreat, embrace the gloom.
Lines unspoken, hearts will sing,
Hidden treasures love can bring.

Words lie dormant, shadows play,
Unseen rhythms mark the day.
In stillness, feelings softly sprout,
Unsaid poetry, lost but stout.

Ink upon the paper's edge,
Promises dance, a silent pledge.
In hushed tones, we dare to dream,
Unsaid poetry flows like a stream.

A gentle touch, a knowing glance,
Between us lives a silent dance.
Where language fails, our hearts collide,
In the unsaid, love abides.

Crafting worlds without a sound,
In the quiet, truth is found.
This unwritten verse, so profound,
In unsaid poetry, we are bound.

The Language of Silence

In silent seas where whispers dwell,
A secret tongue begins to swell.
Words unspoken, softly bind,
The language of silence, intertwined.

Glimmers of thought, a sacred pause,
In quietude, our hearts will cause.
A tale unfolds without a sound,
The language of silence, profound.

Feel the stillness, hear the call,
In silent rooms, we find it all.
Voices echo in the night,
In darkness, our true thoughts take flight.

A shared glance, a fleeting smile,
In the silence, we travel miles.
Words may fail, but love withstands,
The language of silence, hand in hands.

Through gentle sighs and breathless beats,
In quiet moments, the heart repeats.
In this space, the truth ignites,
The language of silence, our shared lights.

The Silence Between Souls

In whispers soft, they tread the night,
Two hearts adrift, in muted light.
A pause so deep, a breath, a sigh,
Their dreams converge, yet none rely.

The world around fades to grey,
As bonds are forged in deep dismay.
No words are spoken, still they feel,
A truth unmasked, a fate revealed.

Moments linger, shadows dance,
With every glance, they take a chance.
The silence hums, it weaves a thread,
Connecting souls with words unsaid.

Each heartbeat echoes, soft yet strong,
In the quiet, they belong.
A language born of glances shared,
In unison, they find they're paired.

Through pauses deep and sighs that blend,
They find a love that knows no end.
In silence rich, within the fold,
Their story whispers, yet remains bold.

Moments Lost to Stillness

Time drifts softly, lost in haze,
As fleeting hours slip away.
A world in pause, the air holds tight,
In silent rooms, the heart takes flight.

The clock unveils a bittersweet tale,
As memories fade, hopes unveil.
Each breath a sigh, each glance a plea,
In moments still, they long to be.

The rustle of leaves, the gentle breeze,
Bring echoes of warmth, like long-lost keys.
Yet shadows creep, and light will wane,
In stillness found, they feel the pain.

Yet hope remains in whispered dreams,
In fleeting thoughts that shatter seams.
Moments lost, yet held so dear,
In silence wrapped, they persevere.

The world spins on, yet here they stay,
In stillness deep, where hearts will play.
Through shadows cast, their spirit soars,
As moments lost unlock new doors.

A Melody of the Unheard

In twilight's glow, a song takes flight,
A melody born of pure delight.
It weaves through dreams, both soft and clear,
An echo found when no one's near.

With every note, the silence hums,
A rhythm soft, where longing comes.
In whispers low, the heart will sing,
Each unheard chord, a secret spring.

The world outside may rush and race,
Yet in this dance, they find their place.
A tapestry of sound and grace,
In fleeting moments, they embrace.

Solitude wraps them in its shroud,
While stars above shine fierce and proud.
In shadows deep, they lose their fear,
For in this song, all truths are clear.

A melody born from love untold,
In hearts entwined, it feels so bold.
Through whispered dreams and starlit skies,
An unheard song that never dies.

The Unseen Dialogues

Between the lines where silence dwells,
Two souls converse in subtle spells.
Their eyes, a canvas, paint the night,
With gestures soft, they share their plight.

The words unsaid, a quiet truth,
In every glance, a loving proof.
As thoughts entwine like ivy's grasp,
In unseen dialogues, they clasp.

Amidst the noise, their hearts beat clear,
In vibrant dreams, they draw so near.
With every sigh, the air is thick—
An intimacy that time can't pick.

The world around may never see,
The bond they hold so tenderly.
In silent vows, their spirits soar,
In hidden realms, they seek for more.

Each fleeting touch, a spark ignites,
In the unseen, their love invites.
With every heartbeat, they confide,
In the unseen dialogues, they bide.

Echoes of the Heart

Whispers linger in the air,
Softly calling, a gentle flare.
Memories dance like shadows in light,
Echoes fade, yet hold on tight.

Time stands still, the heartbeats race,
Each pulse a soft, familiar trace.
Silent stories weaved and spun,
Unraveled threads, yet never done.

In twilight's glow, the secrets hold,
A tapestry of warmth and cold.
In every sigh, in each embrace,
The echoes live, they leave their face.

Life's symphony sings low and bright,
In every shadow, in each light.
Resounding chords of love and pain,
A melody that will remain.

Through the storms and gentle calm,
The heart's echo serves as balm.
In every turn, a path reveals,
Healing whispers, love's appeals.

Innuendo of Emotions

Soft glances exchanged in haste,
Under the moon, a silent taste.
Words unspoken hang in the air,
Hints of feelings, nearly bare.

A brush of hands, electric flame,
Every moment, a tender game.
Eyes collide, a silent plea,
Innuendo flows like a gentle sea.

Laughter echoes, a playful sound,
Beneath the surface, love is found.
A whisper here, a murmur there,
Hidden layers of sweet despair.

Time ticks slowly, hearts race fast,
Every heartbeat shadowed by the past.
Innuendo, like a fleeting ghost,
Holds the truth, yet fears the most.

So let us dance in this twilight hue,
Where unspoken words feel so true.
In this moment, we are so near,
Innuendo speaks what we cannot clear.

Beneath the Veil

Layers woven, secrets kept,
In silence, many truths are swept.
Beneath the veil, shadows reside,
Hopes and fears, they both collide.

A soft touch, a fleeting glance,
Hidden worlds in a whispered dance.
The veil lifts, just for a while,
Revealing dreams wrapped in a smile.

In twilight's embrace, we find our way,
Navigating through shades of gray.
A heartbeat shared, a quiet sigh,
Beneath the veil, where whispers lie.

Yet courage brews in heart's domain,
To lift the veil, to break the chain.
With every truth, a light unfolds,
Beneath the veil, the soul beholds.

So dare to peek, to seek the light,
Beyond the fear, beyond the night.
For what lies there, we must unveil,
A tapestry woven, beneath the veil.

Unvoiced Thoughts

In shadows deep, thoughts intertwine,
Words unsaid, like aged wine.
Bottled feelings, held so tight,
Unvoiced thoughts throughout the night.

A heavy heart, a quiet mind,
In silence, echoes we still find.
Fleeting moments slip away,
Unvoiced thoughts choose to stay.

Each sigh a story, a silent plea,
In the stillness, we hear the sea.
Tides of longing, waves of grief,
Unvoiced thoughts, sweet disbelief.

Two souls connect in whispered air,
In silence shared, we lay bare.
Emotions whirl, a hidden dance,
Unvoiced thoughts seek one last chance.

So speak the truth, let silence break,
In unvoiced thoughts, the heart awakes.
With open lines, and voices clear,
We'll share the weight, and shed the fear.

The Quiet Within

In hushed tones of twilight, we find our peace,
Where shadows dance softly, and worries cease.
A world filled with echoes, yet silence sings,
In the heart's gentle chambers, the stillness clings.

Beneath the moon's gaze, secrets unfold,
In the warmth of the silence, our truths are told.
With every soft breath, the fears drift away,
In this tranquil embrace, we welcome the day.

Through moments of stillness, our spirits entwine,
In the quiet, together, we patiently shine.
A symphony whispered, though none may perceive,
In the depths of our hearts, we truly believe.

As dawn breaks with colors that paint the sky,
We cherish the silence, let worries fly.
In the quiet within, our souls come alive,
With each breath of stillness, we learn to thrive.

Here amidst the calm, love softly calls,
In the embrace of silence, we break down walls.
For when noise subsides, our spirits can soar,
In the heart of the quiet, we find so much more.

Untold Connections

In glances exchanged, through a crowded room,
An energy lingers, dispelling gloom.
Words left unspoken, yet volumes are clear,
A bond that transcends, though we barely draw near.

Through laughter and sighs, unseen threads weave,
Stories of hope that we each can believe.
In the smallest of gestures, a universe blooms,
An untold connection in our heart's empty rooms.

With each fleeting moment, the magic does grow,
An echo of presence that only we know.
In memories cherished, though distant apart,
The fabric of friendship is stitched through the heart.

Our paths may diverge, yet the pulse remains,
In silence and noise, through joys and through pains.
In every heartbeat, a truth we can find,
We are woven together, transcending all time.

Though words may escape us, deep down we feel,
An unbreakable bond that forever is real.
So let us remember, as life's currents flow,
The untold connections that only we know.

Faded Whispers

In the corners of twilight, memories play,
Faded whispers of dreams that slipped away.
The soft sigh of moments, once vibrant and bright,
Now linger like shadows in the hush of the night.

Each echo speaks softly, of laughter and tears,
Of moments we cherished, through smiles and fears.
Though time may have dulled them, their essence remains,
In the quiet of corners, nostalgia refrains.

Through the veil of the past, we reach for the glow,
Of the days we once danced, when we felt the flow.
In the tapestry woven, we find lose threads,
Faded whispers that linger, from what once was said.

With every soft gust, the memories breathe,
In the light of the stars, our hearts still believe.
Though moments have faded, love will not end,
In the whispers of night, our souls still transcend.

For even in silence, our hearts still collide,
In the chambers of longing, where shadows abide.
Faded whispers of love, forever they stay,
Soft echoes of memories that never decay.

Between Heartbeats

In the space between heartbeats, a truth is revealed,
An uncharted journey, where wounds are healed.
In the stillness we find, as the world rushes by,
A moment of magic where silence can fly.

Through whispers of longing, our spirits unite,
In the pause that we share, the world feels just right.
Every beat tells a story, each sigh has its place,
In the realm of connection, we find our embrace.

With every soft heartbeat, a symphony grows,
A rhythm of comfort, where love overflows.
In the heart's gentle cadence, we listen and learn,
Between beats of our souls, the candles still burn.

In the quiet between laughter, in tears that we shed,
Lie the moments of clarity, the words left unsaid.
In the space of our being, we yearn to explore,
The depths of connection, forever wanting more.

So let us dwell softly, in this sacred thrill,
In the heartbeat of life, our souls are fulfilled.
For here in this silence, where time stands apart,
We find all our answers, right here in the heart.

Muted Longings

In shadows deep, my heart does hide,
Whispers soft where dreams reside.
Fingers trace the lines of fate,
Silent wishes hesitate.

The nightingale sings a hushed refrain,
Echoes linger, sweet yet vain.
Lost in thought, time drifts away,
Fleeting stars will not obey.

In daylight's grasp, I seek the light,
Yet shadows cling, veiling the bright.
A candle flickers, hope's soft glow,
Yet still, the longing starts to grow.

The heart can speak in muted tones,
In every sigh, a truth atones.
From depths unknown, I draw my breath,
Between the lines, I dance with death.

To yearn for what may never be,
A paradox of soul set free.
In quiet corners, secrets seep,
Within my soul, the dreams I keep.

Between the Lines

Words unspoken linger in air,
They weave a tale, a whispered dare.
The ink, a river of thoughts to find,
Where truths reside, yet stay confined.

In every pause, a world unfolds,
Stories hidden, yet to be told.
Between the lines, emotions blend,
Silent gestures, a lover's send.

The paper holds the weight of time,
As fleeting moments turn to rhyme.
Imagined paths diverge and meet,
In quiet joy and bitter defeat.

An open book, yet closed to eyes,
A voyage bound by silent ties.
In hallowed space where hearts ignite,
Between the lines lies purest light.

To read the sighs and whispered dreams,
To find the truth in silent screams.
We seek the spaces where they dwell,
Between the lines, all is we tell.

The Unwritten Symphony

In twilight's hush, a song awaits,
Each note a door, to myriad fates.
Silence wraps the strings of night,
An unwritten symphony takes flight.

With every heartbeat, rhythms flow,
A canvas vast of ebb and glow.
Dreams compose in shadowed bars,
While starlit winds weave through the stars.

Each moment breathes a melody,
In echoes wild, they set us free.
In harmony, we find our voice,
In quietude, we make our choice.

The dance of life, a graceful turn,
In whispered chords, our spirits yearn.
Each pause a chance, each breath a space,
An unwritten tune for hearts to chase.

With every note that fades away,
We sculpt a future from the clay.
In silence, dreams begin to play,
In unwritten symphonies, we sway.

Silence Speaks

In the quiet room, whispers bloom,
Embers flicker, casting gloom.
Words unsaid fill the air,
In tender spaces, souls laid bare.

A glance, a sigh, the heart reveals,
In hushed tones, the spirit heals.
Between each breath, truths intertwine,
In silent echoes, love defines.

The world may roar, yet here we stand,
In the stillness, hand in hand.
No need for words, our hearts collide,
In the space where silence abides.

Through quietude, my thoughts take flight,
In the shadows, warmth ignites.
In every pause, a story wakes,
In silence deep, the heart remakes.

To speak is fine, but to be still
Is where the heart finds truest thrill.
In silence speaks the love we claim,
In quiet depths, we find our name.

Shadows in Conversation

In whispers low, where shadows meet,
Their tales entwined, the night discreet.
A dance of forms, in light they play,
Two souls converse, then fade away.

Beneath the stars, they softly glide,
In gentle curves, the secrets bide.
A fleeting glance, a ghostly smile,
Together lost for just a while.

In twilight's hush, they share a sigh,
Moments drift, as time slips by.
Yet every word remains unheard,
In silence deep, what once occurred.

As daybreak breaks, the shadows flee,
Their sacred pact, a mystery.
But in the heart, those echoes stay,
In whispers soft, where shadows play.

Fragments of Silence

In quiet rooms, we learn to wait,
For murmurs lost, we hesitate.
Each breath a note, unheard, untried,
In fragments small, where dreams reside.

The world outside, a distant sound,
Yet here in stillness, peace is found.
Captured moments, like fragile glass,
Reflecting time, as shadows pass.

An empty chair, the dust remains,
A story told, through silent chains.
Echoes linger in every pause,
In fragments held, we find our cause.

Each heartbeat thrums, a whispered plea,
For what was lost, for what could be.
In silence vast, our hopes align,
In fragments small, the world's design.

The Heart's Quiet Cry

Beneath the calm, a tempest brews,
In whispered thoughts, a hidden muse.
Each beat a tale, unspoken, raw,
The heart's own voice, too shy for law.

In midnight's cloak, when all is still,
The pulse reveals what words can't fill.
In starlit silence, dreams collide,
As shadows hold the fears we hide.

A gentle ache, a soft lament,
The heart's quiet cry, in whispers spent.
Each sigh a path to worlds unknown,
In quiet depths, we find our own.

When dawn arrives, and light breaks gray,
The heart retreats, it keeps at bay.
Yet still it beats, a truth untamed,
In quiet cries, our souls are named.

Secrets of the Unvoiced

In shadows cast, where secrets lie,
There blooms a world, too shy to try.
The unvoiced words, like petals fall,
In silent grace, they tell it all.

Amongst the trees, where echoes sleep,
The whispers fade, but still they keep.
Each hidden truth, a silent scream,
In secret paths, we weave a dream.

With every glance, a story shared,
Yet in the still, we're left unpaired.
The quiet souls, they seek to find,
In every pause, what's undefined.

The heart knows well, the dance of fears,
In starlit nights, it sheds its tears.
The secrets held, in shadows cast,
The unvoiced wishes, meant to last.

The Silent Battle Within

In shadows deep, the whispers tread,
Where thoughts collide, and fears are fed.
A war unseen, yet felt so close,
The heart a fortress, pride a ghost.

An inner voice, a constant fight,
Against the dark, to find the light.
With every breath, strength ebbs and flows,
Braving storms, as courage grows.

Through scars and wounds, we learn to stand,
Though life may toss, we hold the strand.
In silence loud, where echoes play,
The battle rages, night and day.

With every tear, a truth unveils,
Amid the dread, the spirit sails.
Though weak at times, we rise once more,
United still, through every war.

For in the quiet, strength does bloom,
Amidst the chaos, we find our room.
A silent fight, so deeply known,
The heart learns how to find its throne.

Hidden Emotions

Beneath the smile, a story hides,
A tapestry of pain that bides.
In muted tones, the heart conceals,
What words can't speak, the spirit feels.

Behind the laughter, shadows dance,
A fragile soul lost in a trance.
Each glance away, a hidden plea,
Yearning for love, to set it free.

In quiet sighs, the truth remains,
A world of joy encased in chains.
Yet in the depths, a flicker glows,
With every storm, the heart still knows.

Through every tear that silent falls,
A whisper calls, as courage sprawls.
To break the chains, to speak the ache,
And in that moment, find the break.

For hidden emotions seek the sun,
In darkness kept, we come undone.
Yet with each step, we learn to shine,
In light embraced, our hearts entwine.

Untouched Voices

In crowded rooms, the silence screams,
Each heart a vessel filled with dreams.
Yet words unspoken fill the air,
With stories longing to declare.

Within the stillness, spirits soar,
Caught in the gaze, we want much more.
But fear holds tight, a heavy thread,
Silencing all the things unsaid.

Eyes meet briefly, then drift apart,
Leaving behind an aching heart.
Untouched voices whisper low,
In every glance, a chance to grow.

For every soul that longs for peace,
In quiet moments, the yearnings cease.
Yet beneath it all, the truths remain,
Silent echoes, a soft refrain.

To find the courage, to pave the way,
To share the song, come what may.
In harmony, we'll find our choice,
To lift the hush, embrace our voice.

Echoes of Silence

In the stillness, echoes sway,
Waves of thoughts that drift away.
Each breath an echo, faint and clear,
Whispers lost, yet always near.

Through the silence, stories weave,
Threads of longing, we believe.
A canvas blank, awaiting strokes,
In quiet spaces, the heart invokes.

With every pause, reflections bloom,
In shadows cast, we find our room.
A gentle pulse, a soft embrace,
In silence held, we find our place.

Though words may fade, the feelings rise,
In echoes held, beneath the skies.
For in the hush, the truth ignites,
In quietude, the soul ignites.

So let the silence speak its mind,
In echoes clear, our hearts aligned.
For in the silence, love's refrain,
We find our hope, we shed our pain.

The Unexpressed Canvas

In shadows deep, a whisper grows,
Colors blend, where no one knows.
A canvas waits, untouched by light,
Dreams unfold in the silent night.

Brushes poised, a gentle hand,
A story waits, yet unplanned.
Each stroke a thought, yet to be shown,
An artist's heart, all alone.

Eyes closed tight, imagination flies,
Amidst the stillness, hope never dies.
A vision sparks within the mind,
In every hue, the lost will find.

Lines of sorrow, traces of joy,
In this silence, truths deploy.
Unseen beauty, waiting to bloom,
In the depths of a quiet room.

The canvas waits for words to spill,
An unexpressed heart, waiting still.
Artistry lingers, beguiled by fate,
In each heartbeat, the world is awake.

Echoes of Untold Love

In the quiet, hearts align,
A rhythm soft, a secret sign.
Two souls dance, in shadows cast,
Echoes linger, memories last.

Unspoken words, a tender glance,
In every chance, the hidden dance.
A gentle hum, beneath the stars,
Love reverberates, near and far.

In twilight's hush, where dreams collide,
The heart knows well, there's nowhere to hide.
Silent vows, with every beat,
In this moment, our worlds complete.

Through whispered thoughts, we're intertwined,
In empty spaces, our hearts remind.
Unrevealed stories, we silently share,
In every breath, love lingers there.

Beyond the night's veil, longing waits,
Each moment real, yet it skates.
An echo of love, pure and true,
In silenced tones, I reach for you.

Soft Narratives

In the stillness, tales unfold,
Soft narratives, gently told.
Whispers weave through the night's embrace,
Every story finds its place.

A fleeting glance, a touch so light,
In quiet echoes, love takes flight.
Between the lines, a truth is found,
Softly spoken, it knows no bound.

In murmurs sweet, the heart will write,
Pages turning, lost in flight.
Through every sigh, each wish proclaimed,
In soft narratives, we are named.

With every breath, a world anew,
Where dreams converge and hope holds true.
Stories linger in the air we share,
Soft narratives speak, where hearts lay bare.

Time ebbs softly, a gentle stream,
In every glance, a shared dream.
An unspoken bond, a timeless thread,
In soft narratives, we dare tread.

Unrevealed Sentiments

In hidden corners, feelings dwell,
Unrevealed sentiments cast a spell.
Beneath the smiles lies a deep sea,
Waves of affection, wild and free.

In silence shared, the heart confides,
Secrets bloom where truth abides.
Each heartbeat echoes, a silent plea,
In unrevealed depths, love's decree.

With every glance, a story flows,
Veiled emotions, only one knows.
Through tender gazes, worlds collide,
Unrevealed sentiments, where hearts abide.

In the shadows, passion hides,
Veiling the light from where it bides.
Yet there it lingers, softly bright,
In every shadow, love ignites.

To speak the words still feels a weight,
But in this silence, we create.
An uncharted realm, emotions swell,
In unrevealed sentiments, all is well.

Milton Keynes UK
Ingram Content Group UK Ltd.
UKHW021954151124
451186UK00007B/249